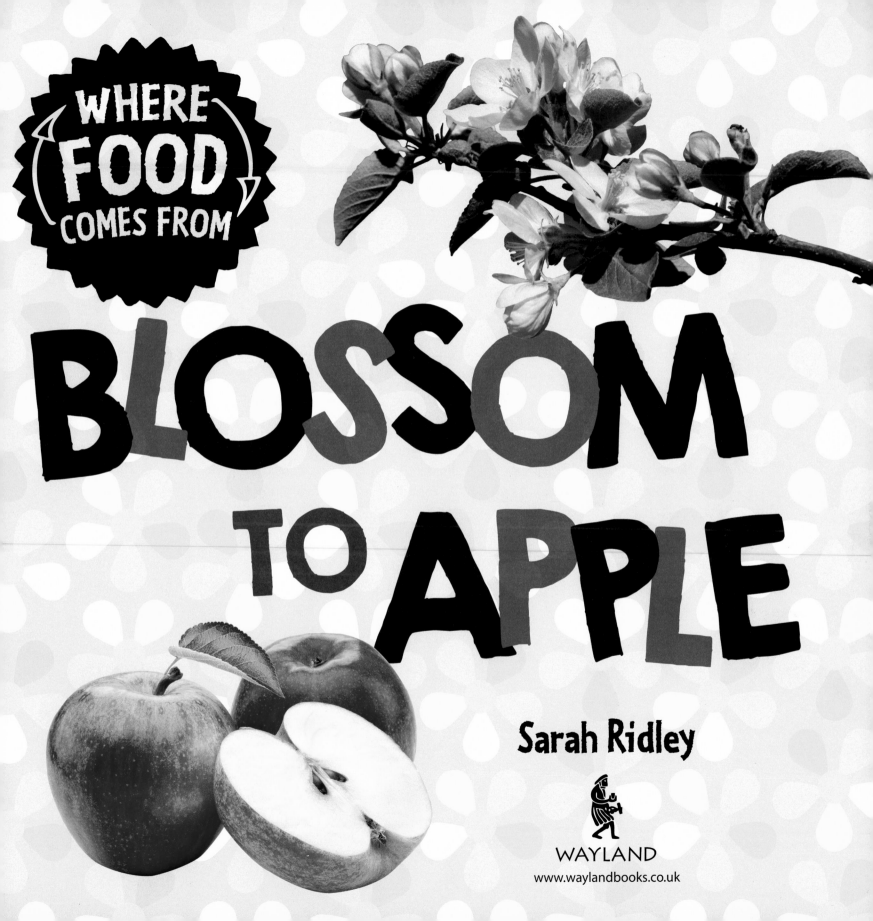

WHERE FOOD COMES FROM

BLOSSOM TO APPLE

Sarah Ridley

WAYLAND
www.waylandbooks.co.uk

First published in Great Britain in 2018
by Wayland
Copyright © Hodder and Stoughton, 2018
Editor: Sarah Peutrill
Designer: Matt Lilly
ISBN: 978 1 5263 0625 8

FSC
www.fsc.org
MIX
Paper from
responsible sources
FSC® C104740

Printed and bound in China
Wayland, an imprint of
Hachette Children's Group
Part of Hodder and Stoughton
Carmelite House
50 Victoria Embankment
London EC4Y 0DZ
An Hachette UK Company
www.hachette.co.uk
www.hachettechildrens.co.uk

Words in bold like **this** are in the glossary on page 24.

Apples are a tasty fruit.

We eat them raw ...

cook them ...

... and squash them to make juice.

But where do apples come from?

3

Apples are the fruit of apple trees.
They grow in gardens or orchards.
Most big orchards belong
to fruit farmers.

4

There are thousands of different varieties of apple tree. Their apples look and taste different.

APPLE FACT

Apple varieties have names. Here are a few: Cox, Bramley, Braeburn, Orange Pippin, Granny Smith and Gala.

5

In winter, apple trees stand bare in the garden or orchard.

APPLE FACT

Apple trees are deciduous, which means they drop their leaves in autumn. Evergreen trees keep their leaves over the winter.

This fruit farmer is pruning his apple trees.
He cuts off dead branches as well as branches
that are growing too close to each other.

As the air warms up in spring, buds swell on the branches of the trees.

bud ➝

leaves

The first buds unfold into small green leaves.

8

Soon after, pink buds open into flowers called blossom.

WONDER WORD:
BLOSSOM

Blossom is another word
for the flowers of trees
or bushes, especially
fruit trees.

9

For a few weeks, apple trees are covered in blossom. The blossom contains a sugary food called nectar.

WONDER WORD:
NECTAR

Nectar is a sweet liquid made by plants to attract insects to their flowers.

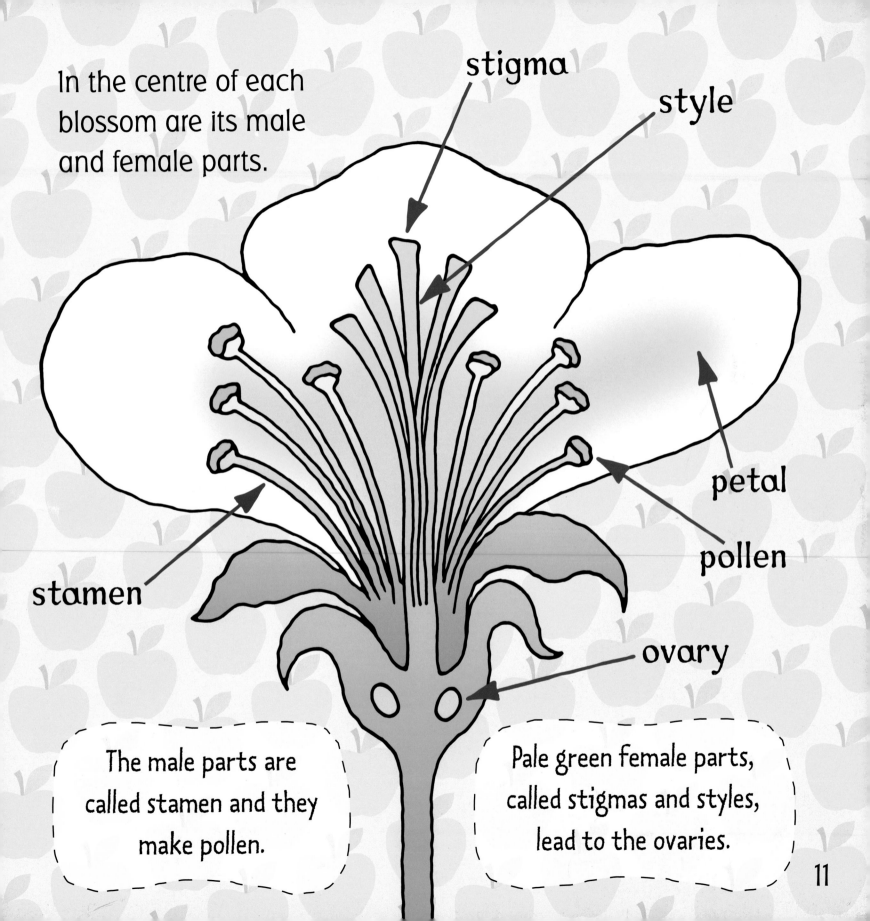

In the centre of each blossom are its male and female parts.

stigma

style

petal

pollen

stamen

ovary

The male parts are called stamen and they make pollen.

Pale green female parts, called stigmas and styles, lead to the ovaries.

On warm, dry days, apple trees buzz with the sound of bees. The bees fly from tree to tree, collecting nectar. Other insects collect the nectar too.

As a bee sucks up nectar, pollen sticks to her hairy body. Some of the pollen brushes off onto the next blossom she visits, allowing pollination to happen.

WONDER WORD:
POLLINATION

Pollination takes place when the male part (pollen) of one flower reaches the female part of another, allowing it to make fruit and seeds.

13

Soon, the blossom petals fall to the ground. Where the blossom once was, tiny apples start to grow and swell.

14

APPLE FACT

In early summer, apple trees lose some of their smallest apples to allow the rest to grow well.

During the summer, the trees are covered in green leaves. The leaves make food for the trees using water, air and sunlight. Water is soaked up by roots under the ground.

The food that reaches the apples makes them grow bigger and bigger. Warmth from the Sun helps apples to ripen in late summer and autumn.

Ripe apples will drop to the ground if we don't pick them first. In the garden, people can pick a ripe apple whenever they want to eat or cook one. An apple is ripe if it comes off the tree with a gentle twist.

Fruit farmers pay pickers
to harvest the apples.
It is a busy time.

18

WONDER WORD:
HARVEST

The gathering of ripe fruit,
vegetables, nuts and grains.

Sometimes pickers need to use a ladder to reach the apples at the top of tall trees.

The pickers carefully place the apples in big crates or boxes.

Many fruit farmers send their apples to packing houses. There, apples are washed, sorted and packed.

The apples are put into bags, boxes or trays.

Farmers sell their apples to shops and
markets, or to factories where the apples are
made into juice, pies and other products.

We buy apples and bring them home to eat. Like other fruit, apples help us to stay healthy as they contain **vitamins** and **minerals**.

If you cut an apple in half you will see its seeds, or pips. You can grow an apple tree from seed but most people plant small trees. Before long, the young apple tree will blossom and grow apples.

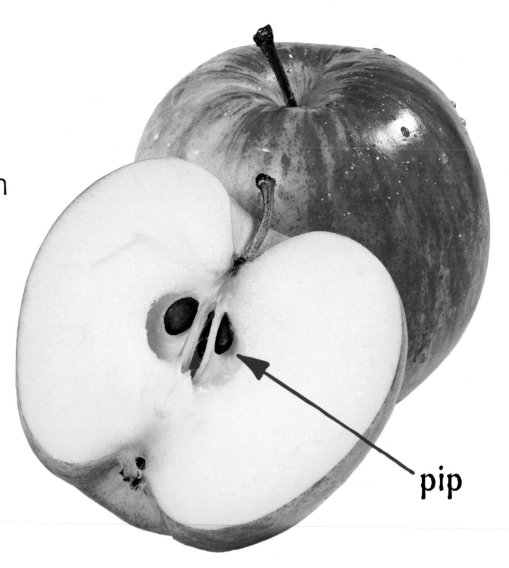

pip

This apple has been cut in half across its widest part. What shape can you see?

GLOSSARY

digest To break down food in the body.

ripe Ready to eat.

vitamins and **minerals** Natural substances found in food which the body needs in small amounts to stay healthy.

INDEX